Spirit, Kingdom and Mission

A Charismatic Missiology

Andrew Lord

Ordinand, Ridley Hall, Cambridge
Formerly Area Co-ordinator for the Church Mission Society

GROVE BOOKS LIMITED
RIDLEY HALL RD   CAMBRIDGE   CB3 9HU

Contents

Acknowledgements

I want to thank my wife Debbie for her support and her inspiration in mission. Could I also thank all in CMS for their encouragement and stimulus to thought in recent years. Thanks also to Gavin Wakefield and John Witcombe for their helpful comments on earlier drafts, and Mark Cartledge for the initial encouragement to write this booklet.

The Cover Illustration is by Peter Ashton

First Impression January 2002
ISSN 1470-8531
ISBN 1 85174 488 6

1
Introduction

The mission of the church began at Pentecost as the gathered disciples were baptized with the Holy Spirit. Mission flowed naturally out of an overpowering experience of God and the fearful few were transformed into witnesses of Christ to the ends of the earth. A new and ever expanding mission community was formed, characterized by signs and wonders, practical sharing, teaching and worship. The community was later scattered and formed new communities as the church travelled in mission across the world.

Any attempt to understand and practise mission in the church today needs to draw on the rich tradition of Pentecost. The Pentecostal and charismatic movements have been particularly influenced by the vision and experience of Pentecost. Yet I want to suggest in this booklet that we have reached a point in our journey where we need God to extend our understanding of mission. It can sometimes feel that our mission is concerned with the 'spiritual,' separate from the practical realities of daily life. A division between the church and the world can be unconsciously cultivated in ways that can ultimately leave mission disconnected from life. This is often encouraged by an over-focus on evangelism and 'the lost' which leaves the wider aspects of mission untouched. The move in some quarters to social and ecological involvement is not always easy to connect with evangelism. Wider issues surround the role of the local church, with a tendency to define the local church (or cell) as the almost exclusive agent of mission. This can give a healthy impetus to the mission of the church but can easily exclude mission in the workplace and lead to a congregationalism that ignores the wider movements of mission. We need ways of holding the local and the universal aspects of mission together in a way that enriches both.

In all these things the all-embracing power and creativity of Pentecost can be lost, leaving people wondering what the challenge of mission has to do with them. A deeper and wider understanding of the Holy Spirit and the kingdom of God can help us extend our missiology and our understanding and practice of mission. This booklet outlines a charismatic missiology that is both experiential and holistic, attempting to overcome unhealthy divisions and connect mission in a holistic way with everyday life. It is a missiology that is practised by a diverse range of mission communities within the universal church as they catch the vision of the Spirit. My prayer is that as we encounter the Spirit in ever deeper ways we may be more open to the breadth of God's vision for mission and sent by him in new ways into the world.

2
Experiential Mission

At the heart of any charismatic missiology is experience. It is the experience of the woman who finds Christ and through him finds her life transformed. It is the experience of the man whose encounter with Christ leads him to change the way he approaches his management at work. It is the experience of a community torn apart by tragedy which is drawn together in worship of the one who suffered and died before rising again. The practice of mission is discovered in the ordinary as the Spirit points us to God's transforming power. The biblical understanding of the Spirit, particularly in the Old Testament, directs us to see a strong link between the Spirit and life. Hence Jesus says, 'it is the Spirit that gives life' (John 6.63) and the Nicene creed summarizes that the Spirit is the 'Lord and giver of life.' Jürgen Moltmann has done much to direct us to explore in a deeper way the link between the Spirit and experience. For him the Spirit is the 'power of life in all the living' who also confronts us with God's presence.[1]

Transforming the Ordinary

An experience of the Holy Spirit is one that relates the power of God to our ordinary lives, work, communities and culture. From the three thousand who responded to Christ on the day of Pentecost, the book of Acts brims with experiences of healings and exorcisms, of changed lives and communities, of a people encountering God wherever they went. Today this seems far from the average experience of even charismatic churches and the challenge remains as to how we can see the experience of God at the centre of our mission. The Old Testament reminds us that the Spirit is not limited to church on a Sunday. The Spirit also gifts people with creativity in their daily work. Yet, as one man said to me recently, 'our church does nothing that is relevant to my work.' Another complained, 'Why does the church aim to take up more and more of my time—don't they know I have a pressured job?' Increased pressures in the workplace coupled with a view of mission that just places more pressure on people is hardly likely to bring life and joy. Growing churches tend to be those that either relate well to the local community or form an alternative community which people often travel to join. In the latter case, although the church grows it can often relate little to its immediate community, which can feel abandoned by the church. We cannot escape the challenge to relate to our community, and we can see signs of this in the

---

1   Jürgen Moltmann, *The Spirit of Life* (London: SCM, 1992).

provision of services of healing and meditation, courses on parenting, involvement in local action groups, provision of debt counselling, and so on. As John V Taylor suggested, the Holy Spirit is the 'go-between God' who aims to bring our God, our work and our community together.[2]

Renewed Imagination

We need to think what steps we can take that will see us better empowered by God and more able to engage in our workplaces and communities. Our starting point needs to be a deepening of our experience of God in prayer and worship. In this we might usefully pick up on the work of Brueggemann on prophetic imagination.[3] He sees the Scriptures primarily in terms of their rhetorical ability to generate an imagination that runs counter to the present-day reality of the faithful. Although he applies this approach to the Old Testament we can usefully apply it to the narrative found in Acts. In a situation where a dynamic mission of 'signs and wonders' seems far from our reality there is a need to develop an imagination that sees these as more natural. From this imagination can spring, under the Spirit, a changed reality that is more in line with God's vision for mission. Such an approach can be seen in the life of John Wimber who preached for months on the desire of God to heal before any healing took place. He was committed to preaching God's counter-reality until it became more the every-day reality of the congregation's life. The use of testimony is also vital here; the stories of ordinary people encountering the powerful God inspiring others to see the world more through the eyes of God. It was an imagination full of the scriptural testimonies to God that enabled the early church to face persecution in Acts 4. Here the church gathered in prayer to affirm the nature of God and the reality of opposition as testified to in the Scriptures. This gave the basis for a bold prayer for 'signs and wonders' that later were demonstrated. Of course, it is not the case that getting our imagination fired up will immediately lead to experiencing the power of God. We need to be open to the power of God through weakness, but without such imagination our expectations are lowered and the *status quo* becomes acceptable.

Experience of God

A renewed imagination formed in the context of prayer and worship needs to be carried into the mundane of everyday life because that is the place of mission. This is difficult in a context where 'the sense of God is vanishing from the earth' (Pope John Paul II). The divide between work and worship seems so great, and yet it needs to be overcome. Two possible ways forward

2   John V Taylor, *The Go-Between God: The Holy Spirit and the Christian Mission* (London: SCM, 1972).
3   Walter Brueggemann, *Theology of the Old Testament* (Fortress Press, 1997) pp 53-71.

can be seen in the recognition of 'annunciations' and an appreciation of the role of the Spirit in ethics. John V Taylor starts his exploration of the role of the Holy Spirit in mission with a consideration of the 'annunciations' that are common to all people. Thus a spectacular sunset can leave people feeling they have experienced something beyond themselves, which they may talk of as a 'spiritual experience.' Conversely, at times of pain people may feel their own limitations and the brokenness of the world and from within this pain reach out to God and experience a 'strange comfort' in the midst of despair. Such experiences, if recognized and valued, can become stepping stones to more distinctive experiences and understandings of the Triune God. At a recent baptism preparation meeting the discussion seemed to be coming to a halt. I asked a question only to get silence in return. I noticed one lady whom the Spirit seemed to indicate had something to say. When prompted, she gave an unexpected testimony about the way God met with her after her father's death. This then gently opened up into a discussion about the importance of experiencing God and how we might seek God better.

Hidden Powers

In previous work for a multinational company I remember how important it was to keep quietly open to Spirit-prompted conversations. One man opened up about his wife's involvement in a Hindu sect and his own questioning about religion. I had many conversations with another man about the nature of his spiritualist involvement. Our first conversation included the startling fact that he knew things about me that I had not told anyone at work—spiritual forces are as real in the workplace as anywhere else! Often such forces are seen only indirectly through the power-plays that go on in any workplace. These may involve the manipulations seemingly required to hold on to jobs, the fixing of the books, the late payment of invoices, the unfair dismissals, and so on. In this the power of the Spirit in the ethical life is key for Christians. There is a need for a transparent power, humility and integrity that faces evil with love. Such a mission of ethical love can lead to positive changes in the workplace, but is hazardous. It is quite possible that a mission of loving truth could lead to a person being overlooked for promotion or becoming the first in line for redundancy. For the church to support mission in the workplace, it needs both the confidence of the Spirit and the care of the Spirit that is willing to support those ready to risk so much. Currently I know one Christian who has just successfully contested a corrupt effort to make him redundant, and another who faces possible redundancy for being willing to tackle issues surrounding a paedophile. Are we ready to support such people with the cost that such support may bring?

There is nothing that generates a heart for mission more than constant contact with non-Christian realities. We cannot expect mission to happen in a church that is cut off from people outside its own culture and community. As well as encountering things that are far from God's plans we can also discover in our communities examples of 'annunciations.' These are seen both in particular experiences but also in slowly developing outlooks that are in line with what we would equate to 'kingdom values.' Here the Spirit may have been working over years to inspire people in accord with God's kingdom, even if they did not know this. Thus in one parish in Coventry I found a shared concern in the church and community over the abuse of drugs and drink by young people. Reflecting back, this seems an example which could have formed the basis for common mission action within the community, although I was probably too church-focused to realize this at the time. Prayer walks and community surveys can also be ways of developing the skill of prophetic listening so our mission can better connect with the world. In many different ways we need to attempt to ground our mission in experience—the experience of God, our own experience and the experience of those around us. It is the Spirit who brings such experiences together and gives us the discernment required for understanding our particular call to mission.

3
Holistic Mission

In charismatic missiology our experience needs to be permeated by experiences of the kingdom of God. Jesus came preaching that the 'kingdom of God is at hand' and demonstrated the reality of that kingdom in his own life and mission. The kingdom came as people responded to Jesus' challenge to repent and follow him; it came as people were healed of their diseases; it came as Jesus shared food with the ostracized of society; it came as Jesus chose twelve diverse disciples to work together; it came as Jesus valued and transformed creation. God's kingdom is holistic in nature and global in scope and it came in Jesus as the 'Spirit of the Lord' was upon him (Luke 4.18). Mission involves extending the kingdom of God and therefore must by definition be holistic and global, empowered by the Spirit.

Experiencing the Holy Spirit should drive us out with a passion for the holistic kingdom that longs for the world to be valued and transformed. It was such a vision that inspired a small group of unknown worshippers led by William Seymour in Los Angeles early last century. That group became the centre of the Pentecostal movement that quickly spread round the world, extending God's kingdom in the power of the Spirit. The key to this mission seems to have been a deep hunger for God's Spirit and his kingdom. Such hunger was evident in the early church as the disciples asked Jesus, 'Lord, are you at this time going to restore the kingdom to Israel?' (Acts 1.6) They may not have understood what the kingdom was fully about, but they knew that they wanted it! Maybe this can give hope to us as we struggle to turn our churches to look outwards in mission. We can so often feel like the 'unknown few' who struggle to understand the kingdom and who seem overwhelmed by the needs of the church and society. People often acknowledge the need for mission, but feel weighed down by their many other commitments. In so many of the churches that I have visited to talk about mission people have taken me aside to affirm how great it is that people like myself are involved in mission. But when asked about their own mission involvement such people often became slightly lost for words—it is good that someone else is doing the mission but I am not sure of my part! Sometimes people feel that mission is for those in other countries, for evangelists, for the clergy, for those with the time or simply for the keen. We need to find a way of transforming a general acknowledgement of the need for mission into a personal hunger for the kingdom and the Spirit. In developing such a hunger we need to remember the holistic nature of the kingdom. For many people mission means evangelism, and because they do not feel good at evangelism they do not feel enabled to be involved in mission. This leads to guilty inaction rather than Spirit-affirmed action. Steps towards a transformed involvement in mission are often achieved only slowly. We need to continually hold before people a biblical vision of kingdom mission alongside the encouragement of stories illustrating the reality of that vision in practice today.

A Vision of the Kingdom

I have already noted the tendency to define mission solely in terms of evangelism. This seems a particular tendency within some charismatic circles, although the evangelical debate regarding the relationship between evangelism and social action has helped widen outlooks. Jesus' own vision for his ministry and mission is set out in his proclamation at Nazareth in Luke 4.14–21. It is seen in terms of 'preaching good news,' 'proclaiming freedom,' 'recovery of sight,' 'release' and 'the year of the Lord's favour.' It is a holistic kingdom mission agenda that needs to be reflected in the life of the church.

The kingdom has a future as well as a present dimension and I have found it useful to dwell on this future fulfilment in motivating mission in the present. As Robert Warren has commented, 'Today's culture is in particular need of beginning at the End...For we live without hope, direction or purpose.'[4] It is a good challenge to ask people what their vision of mission is—what do they hope to see coming into reality as a result of the church's mission? A constantly stimulating practice in a diocesan evangelism committee I was involved with was for each member of the committee in turn to share at the beginning of a meeting a biblical passage that motivated them in evangelism. From this simple practice of regular testimony came a greater closeness between members of the group and a better shared vision for helping encourage evangelism in the diocese. For me, the passage I have returned to again and again is that of Revelation 7.9–17 which speaks powerfully both of the presence of God and the present reality of suffering. Here is a vision of a people from all over the world centred on God and his salvation in Christ. It is also a vision of the final liberation of a suffering people. The following lines always leave me longing for future healing and present change:

'Never again will they hunger; never again will they thirst.
The sun shall not beat upon them, nor any scorching heat.
For the Lamb at the centre of the throne will be their shepherd;
he will lead them to streams of living water.
God will wipe away every tear from their eyes.' (Rev 7.16–17)

---

4   Robert Warren, *Building Missionary Congregations* (London: Church House Publishing, 1995) p 18.

Looking more widely at the biblical vision of the future kingdom we see a number of themes that characterize the kingdom. It is a kingdom without suffering or death (Rev 7.16–17; 21.4) and a place of healing (Rev 22.1–5). It is a place where God rules (1 Cor 15.24–28; Rev 11.15) and we will be with God, seeing him, knowing him face-to-face and worshipping him (Rev 21.3; Rev 22.4; 1 Cor 13.2; Rev 22.3). All things will be united in Christ (1 Jn 3.2), sharing in his glory (Rom 9.18; Rev. 4.21) and our life together will be like a banquet or wedding feast (Luke 14.15–24; Mt 25.10). Such details fit with the Old Testament prophecies that we often apply to our understanding of heaven, the kingdom to come. One prophecy speaks of a time when 'the wolf also shall dwell with the lamb, and the leopard shall lie down with the kid; and the calf and the young lion and the fatling together; and a little child shall lead them' (Isaiah 11.6). The whole of creation will be brought together in glorious freedom (Rom 8.19–21). Stephen Travis suggests that the coming kingdom will be universal, peaceful and a kingdom of justice and love.[5]

I want to suggest that such a vision of the future kingdom offers a challenge to engage in holistic mission. In mission we are challenged to extend the kingdom in all its fullness in the power of the Spirit. The following five characteristics of the future kingdom suggest a holistic understanding of mission with which to challenge our churches today:

1. People acknowledging Jesus as Lord	Evangelistic mission
2. Healing without suffering or death	Healing mission
3. Perfect justice and peace	Social mission
4. Unity in a diversity of people	Reconciling mission
5. Creation set free	Ecological mission

Two other characteristics of the future kingdom illustrate key aspects in the life of a church that make a good basis for mission, although not themselves a part of that mission:

6. Praise and worship	Christian spirituality
7. Love and fellowship	Christian character and relationships

These two lists can be used as the basis for evaluating the current mission of churches and offering a framework for a more holistic mission. This emphasis on the future kingdom is in line with the 'eschatological urgency' found in Pentecostal missiology—a belief that the end is near and that Christ's re-

---

5   S I I Travis, *I Believe in the Second Coming of Jesus* (London: Hodder & Stoughton, 1982).

turn is imminent. This gives Pentecostals an urgency to proclaim the kingdom to the world before the end comes (Mt 24.14). However, it does not seem to me to be necessary to stress the imminence of Christ's return in order to value the importance of this eschatological vision. The contrast between this vision and the present reality can be a strong motivator for mission, as long as we can see evidence that the present reality is being changed in the direction of this mission.

The Reality of the Kingdom

Our church, like many others, has been involved in distributing copies of the *Jesus* video around the parish. Teams put flyers through letterboxes and followed up with personal visits to offer people the video. Later those who have accepted the video are visited and asked about their response to what they have seen. All of this has been supported by prayer. An encouraging number have taken the video, but it has been more difficult following those people up—often they are out or have not got round to watching the video. Frustration runs alongside hopeful encouragements in the often slow slog of mission. But sometimes things can happen much quicker. One friend, Mary, recently testified to an encounter which led to an unexpected opening. A young lady sat next to her on a seat in town. The lady turned and said how fearful she was. When Mary asked why, she came out with the story of how a friend of similar age had died in the last week and she had just realized that morning how life would not carry on forever. She explained how she did not really believe in God and did not know where Jesus fitted in, but she wanted to know. This sudden opportunity for Mary to share Christ resulted in a good conversation and the lady going away with a tract.

Mission can be seen as the work of the Spirit to bring a foretaste of the future kingdom into the world today—the Spirit is the 'first-fruits' of what is to come (Rom 8.23). Our job is to work with the Spirit in mission that the kingdom may grow and Christ be exalted as Lord. Sometimes the Spirit breaks into our experience and moves mission forward quickly; at other times the Spirit works gradually to grow the kingdom. The history of mission is characterized by a tension between these two modes of the Spirit working. Sometimes a desire for the *inbreaking Spirit* is met and we see God powerfully at work. Other times we struggle more to see the work of the *growing Spirit* working in the background of our mission programs. Mission is ultimately God's and we cannot determine how the Spirit may work, but rather we need to follow the Spirit's lead always in the hope of the change our God can and will bring.

The centre of our mission is Christ who brings all things together. In an Alpha group I once helped to lead was a man who had been widowed the previous year and naturally struggled with grief. Yet soon after one of the

annual memorial services that our church held he met with God in a powerful way in his home. From this came a hunger for Jesus which meant he
readily absorbed the teaching on the Alpha course. His willingness to learn
was a source of encouragement and inspiration to the group. For him, a hunger for Jesus also brought healing in the midst of grief. Such personal healing
happened in the context of the healing community of the church. I remember
another lady who was widowed after the early death of her husband and
who was left to bring up their son alone. The church became her family,
through personal prayer, the homegroup, services and a yearly holiday with
others. Here was a gradual path of healing over many years that seemed to
give her a radiance and a sensitivity to the pain of others. We are called to be
a healing community in mission, one that brings wholeness into the lives of
individuals and parishes. The Spirit who brooded over the creation (Gen 1)
longs to bring glimpses of the re-creation into our lives.

Healing and Reconciling

Healing cannot take place in isolation from others, and involvement in
one kind of mission will always have knock-on effects for other kinds of
mission. Even sudden individual healings can change the dynamics of life
for a family or church. In evangelistic or healing mission we cannot ignore
the social dimensions implicit in any such mission. I have been involved in
an outreach service in a local school that meets each week during term-time
on a Sunday afternoon. This is situated near the council estate in the parish.
In a friendly atmosphere of coffee, cakes and children's activities an all-age
presentation is given. Last term included a very creative presentation of the
gospel entitled 'Toy story—God's story.' In getting to know people it soon
becomes clear that there is a great need for personal healing which cannot be
separated from the social needs of the area. One step out in mission has
broadened our horizons and made us realize afresh the holistic nature of
mission.

The particular social issue of reconciliation is important in Christian mission. The early church wrestled with reconciling Jews and Gentiles within
one community, seeing in Christ the one who broke down the dividing wall
of hostility between the two groups (Eph 2.11–22). The early days of the Pentecostal movement under William Seymour saw people of different races
drawn together to share in the power of God. It is by the Spirit that Christians are born and drawn together into one body in Christ. The work of the
Spirit in reconciling mission is rich and varied: bringing together different
tribes in the Sudan; building understanding and trust between Palestinians
and Jews; enabling Protestants and Catholics to worship and pray together
in Ireland; helping local churches to work together ecumenically; healing
broken relationships within congregations. In many ways our lives, commu-

nities, nations and our world have been broken apart and are in need of the reconciling power of the Spirit.

Paul talks of the groaning of creation in a way that seems to reflect such brokenness (Rom 8.18–25). The field for mission and the effects of mission embrace the whole created order. Ecological mission reflects a concern for the brokenness of creation and a longing for wholeness that re-integrates all things. It is a concern that cannot be separated from the other aspects of mission, as is illustrated by the work of A Rocha in Britain. Here a group of people are working in a difficult area of West London to renew the environment. This involves social involvement with local communities and authorities coming out of a commitment to the God who created the whole universe.[6]

In our mission we are trying in different ways to follow the Spirit in tasting something of the kingdom to come. In this the worship represented by our actions outside church services becomes better united with the worship of our hearts inside church. The God we worship in the Lord Jesus is demonstrated as such in the lives we live and the effect we have in the world. In my experience it has been much easier to challenge people to mission in churches where the worship seems to better encompass the reality of God. Where hearts have been opened to the greatness of God people also seem more receptive to the implications of this for the world. If our mission sometimes seems a struggle then perhaps addressing our worship will show the way forward. How often do we split our mission into the 'mission group' which plans and intercedes, and our church services that worship? Both need elements of worship, intercession and practical vision in order for the mission of the church to grow.

Opposition to the Kingdom

Through worship, fellowship, study and prayer we need to keep our vision of holistic mission nurtured. But in doing so we also need to acknowledge the pressures and opposition that come with any call to mission. The same day that Jesus spoke of his great mission in a synagogue in Nazareth, people rushed to try to throw him off a hill (Luke 4.14–30). Sometimes it can seem that the moment we set out on something new, fired up by a God-given vision, something comes to dampen our enthusiasm and mess up our plans. It is at times like this that the teaching of James and Peter on perseverance and trial seem more deeply relevant (Jas 1.2–12; 1 Pet 1.3–9). As in other areas of our Christian life, opposition to mission can be seen as coming from the world, the flesh and the devil. Sometimes things seem to go against us in a way that simply reflects the fallen nature of the world; things that should be sorted quickly becoming frustratingly difficult to arrange. Sometimes in

---

6   Dave Bookless, 'A Greener, Cleaner Southall and Hayes' *Anglicans for Renewal* 86 (2001) pp 10-12.

mission we become painfully aware of our own failings or those of others. I will always remember a PCC meeting at which one strong personality tried to push his approach to evangelism against the different views of other church leaders. Such situations hinder the development of mission until relationships have been healed. Sometimes we find in mission that forces are at work that go beyond the fallen nature of people and the world; prayerful discernment and historical research may point to the existence of evil forces in an area that are actively at work against the church.

The responses to opposition to kingdom mission will vary depending on the situation, but I would suggest that a holistic approach is required. Our first feelings may be those of weakness and frustration, requiring us to turn to a prayer in the Spirit characterized by groaning (Rom 8.26). Gordon Fee suggests that such groaning relates to praying in tongues which also helps envelop difficulties in the presence of God. This may also lead to tears, as it did for the apostle Paul as he laboured to enable the church in Ephesus to grow (Acts 20.19). Where we become aware of personal failings there is a need to seek a personal transformation that will in some way reflect the transformation of the world we are aiming at in mission. We cannot look outwards in mission to transform what is bad 'out there' without also recognizing what is bad 'in here.' The need for humility is vital in mission, particularly in a situation where many are sensitive to the imperialistic mistakes of the past. There is always a temptation to feel that 'we have it' and 'they need it' without an acknowledgement of the common need we all share for the grace of God. From such a position of humility we can then face the task of so-called 'spiritual warfare.' Much has been written on this subject which is popular in current charismatic missiology through writers such as C Peter Wagner, based on an outlook of kingdoms in conflict. There is not space to enter into this debate here and I just want to stress the need for careful, thought-out, prayerful spiritual discernment of the nature of the evil forces opposing our mission. This can then lead to a program of prayer that is always open to further insights and the possibility of having got it wrong. As our mission encounters opposition we need to develop a patient endurance that recognizes the complexity of our world and the struggles in the Spirit for a transformation of the whole of creation.

A World-wide Kingdom

Mission is holistic in nature, but also holistic geographically. We cannot restrict the mission of God to our particular situation but are challenged, as Jesus challenged the disciples, to see mission as encompassing all the nations. The church around the world shares a *koinonia* (fellowship) in Jesus Christ. Within this 'fellowship of the Holy Spirit' the Spirit distributes gifts as he decides (2 Cor 13.14). What Paul talks about in the context of the local church is also true of the world-wide church: that 'to each one of us grace has been given as Christ apportioned it' (Eph 4.7). The history of the Pentecostal and charismatic movements testifies to the global nature of the Spirit's outpouring, spread through the sharing of spiritual gifts from town to town and country to country. Thus we should not expect all the resources for mission to be available locally. Sometimes this goes against the grain and I remember one vicar of a charismatic church demanding what I, as a representative of a mission society, had to offer that they did not already have. If mission is the responsibility of the local church then should we not get on with it rather than ask others to do it? Yet, I suggest, we need a wider understanding of fellowship and the gifting of the Spirit. It can be easier to give than to receive, and yet we need to look for 'co-workers' in the Spirit who can aid us in our mission and in whose mission we can share. Each church has both gifts and needs which demand a wider partnership in mission. Such partnership is the basis for the work of many mission agencies today and needs to form a part of local church mission practice.[7]

Lichfield diocese has been doing some very creative mission work by linking the mission of local churches with people from the link dioceses in Malaysia, Canada, Germany and South Africa. On a number of occasions teams of people have come to work alongside local churches in specific weeks of mission. This has been a transforming experience for people and churches as they have been invigorated and challenged by others in the task of mission. The receiving of other gifts has led to the growth of gifts and vision locally. One year nearly 300 people came to the diocese from around the world and this has left a legacy of vision for a church that spans the world and in which mission is important. People have also travelled from Lichfield diocese out in mission to the link dioceses and found their vision challenged. One older (theologically 'liberal') church leader shared how his ministry had been transformed since a visit to Malaysia—he now wanted to commit the rest of his ministry to the task of evangelism.

We need to find new and creative ways of enabling a world-wide kingdom mission empowered by the Spirit. Such ways will involve a deepening of fellowship with others around the world and a greater sharing and receiving of gifts. This will not happen in the simple 'missionary pattern' of the past but will require a more flexible approach based on mission movements of the Spirit.

---

7   For details of such approaches within Anglican missiology see Eleanor Johnson and John Clark, eds, *Anglicans in Mission: A Transforming Journey* (London: SPCK, 2000) pp 65-67, 80-81. Tim Dakin is currently developing the idea of 'co-workers' in the mission of CMS.

4
Mission Communities

Charismatic missiology emphasizes the combination of community with movement, rather as a boat set free on the ocean combines an identifiable group of people on the boat with an unavoidable movement caused by the wind and waves. The Spirit brings us together into one community as well as being the wind that 'blows wherever it pleases' (1 Cor 13.12; John 3.8). The practical enabling of holistic kingdom mission requires us to discern where the Spirit is forming or has formed mission communities, and where the Spirit may be leading those communities next. This may be rather like what happened in the church of Antioch which found during a particular time of prayer and fasting that the Spirit spoke words of mission movement: 'Set apart for me Barnabas and Saul for the work to which I have called them' (Acts 13.2). When the two set out they soon faced opposition from a sorcerer, some Jews and city leaders. And yet more people came to believe in Christ, fragile new communities were formed and the kingdom of God continued to advance.

The emphasis on mission *communities* has been of increasing significance in recent missiology. This is, in part, in reaction to approaches to mission that seem simply to involve individuals bringing Christ into the lives of other individuals. Yet if we ask people in local churches about who is interested in mission then we are usually pointed towards certain individuals who have particular links with mission societies or local projects. Rather than realizing that the whole community of the church is involved in mission, we can be pointed to particular people who appear to carry the calling for the rest. An emphasis on the Spirit requires that we see all people, individually but more specifically as communities, as being called to the task of mission—the primary agents of mission are communities rather than individuals. It also requires us to see that part of the result of mission is the formation of new communities. This still seems to go against the grain of popular understanding of missionaries. I visited one church who supported an evangelistic missionary in Kenya. The people were very keen to hear more about his work but seemed to know very little about the church in Kenya, let alone the wider social issues people face in that country. A focus on individuals often blinds us to the need to appreciate the wider communities that are vital in mission. However, a focus on community alone is not sufficient because it can leave our mission too static and comfortable. In Acts we see God regularly interrupting the life of communities to suggest new directions in mission. Our churches should be always characterized by exciting mission initiatives, yet so often they are characterized by memories of the past or initiatives that lack life. The question is how we can keep moving forward in the Spirit.

Spirit-formed Mission Communities

It is not often realized that a key characteristic of Anglican missiology is the work of the Spirit in motivating movements of mission. In particular the mission societies were originally new communities formed by people who felt a common call by God to particular forms of mission. Such communities comprised of people from many different places whom the Spirit had called and gifted to work together in the furtherance of God's kingdom. The world-wide distribution of the Spirit's gifts that we commented on earlier was made concrete in particular dispersed missionary communities. The basis of such communities is generally agreed to be found in the 'voluntary principle' which I have suggested elsewhere can be usefully summarized as follows:[8]

It is the Holy Spirit, working in the hearts of individual believers, who motivates the work of Christian mission.

The challenge of this apparently simple assertion can be seen in three implications that continue to challenge deeply the practice of mission:

1. Mission arises out of an experience of God, rather than just human concern or analysis of the cultural context or even biblical interpretation;
2. Mission is the domain of every believer, not limited to any particular class of person such as clergy or missionaries;
3. Mission is primarily motivated without reference to church organizations—that is to say, mission is primarily a 'bottom-up' rather than a 'top-down' activity.

It can be very easy to try to encourage Christians to mission by calling on them to care more, or to realize the needs of society more, or to realize the scriptural demands of mission. For church leaders these often seem the obvious approaches, and are of value, but they miss out on encouraging experiences of our missionary God. It is the experience of God in worship and through preaching that has initiated many new moves in mission, and it is only mission based firmly on God's call, personally experienced, that will enable mission to positively flourish. We need to think about how our churches can enable people better to encounter God in a way that clarifies their call to mission. This will not be about the church leaders telling the congregation

8   Andrew Lord, 'The Voluntary Principle in Pentecostal Missiology' *Journal of Pentecostal Theology* 17 (2000) pp 81-95.

which mission activities they should be supporting; this can just build guilt or resentment. It is about finding ways that both individuals and the whole community can come before God and receive his word for mission. In one church I was involved in half-nights of prayer that culminated in a time of listening prayer; these were key to the development of sustainable mission initiatives.

The experience of the Pentecostal-charismatic movement has led to an appreciation of three further implications of the voluntary principle:

4. Experiences of God continue to characterize mission and enable continued motivation, as evidenced in 'signs and wonders';
5. Mission is the domain of those on 'the margins' as well as the prosperous and powerful;
6. Mission involves the formation of indigenous Christian communities, rather than communities characterized by foreign cultural practices.

In receiving God's call to mission we need to be open to spiritual gifts and 'signs and wonders' in helping us discern the Spirit's call. It is particularly important to be open to those who may be considered on 'the margins' of our churches. Tom Smail's characterization of the charismatic movement in Britain as 'middle-class Pentecostalism' still carries some reality. It may well take patience and encouragement to enable some people in our churches to hear God and for what they have heard to be valued by those who are better qualified or are more gifted leaders. And before we jump straight into mission planning after discerning the Spirit's leading we need to be aware that we are not called just to copy something that has been done elsewhere in the past. It can be tempting when we hear of new approaches to mission and see videos of remarkable church growth to hope that the same thing will work for us. Yet we need to let the Spirit adapt such insights as appropriate for our situation, developing indigenous approaches rather than approaches that will feel foreign.

Mission Communities and the Church

So far we have been approaching the concept of mission communities in the context of understanding the church as a local congregation. Here the challenge is for congregations to see themselves as mission communities called to be involved in different aspects of a holistic kingdom mission as guided by the Spirit. This challenge has been powerfully put by Robert Warren and others in terms of making the shift from 'maintenance' to 'mission.' Rather than repeat material that is covered well elsewhere I want here to question the simple equation between mission communities and local congregations. The danger with focusing on our own local congregations is that we can think that we 'have it all' and do not need anyone else. I want to suggest that we need an outlook that embraces a plurality of mission communities that may well overlap. Some of these communities may be based in a local area, some over a diocese, some over a country, and some round the world. We should expect the work of the Spirit in mission to give birth to communities of many forms, often not neatly fitting together in an ordered pattern. Every Christian needs encouragment to find out which mission communities the Spirit is moving them to become part of, or to found.

Some examples of possible mission communities might help ground this idea more. In a local church setting many of us have become familiar with the practice of church planting. One church I belonged to was housed in a building that was nowhere near the two centres of population in the Parish. Much prayer and patient waiting was practised to consider which way the church might develop in its outreach. Eventually it was decided to commission a group of about 50 people to plant a new congregation in a local school. This, of course, also meant the re-planting of a new congregation in the existing church building. Two new mission communities were formed that have had to face many difficult mission issues, and I am glad to hear that the plant is still going strong more than 10 years later. Sometimes the mission community is one formed from within a local congregation for a specific mission project. The outreach service in a school that I mentioned earlier is one such example. In this case many people belong to two mission communities—the local congregation and the mission outreach team.

The traditional 'mission prayer group' can also be re-envisioned as a mission community. In a church context, here again is a community within a community. The important thing is to keep the two communities connected—so often mission prayer groups comprise a few who are out of touch with the heart of the rest of church life. The need is for mission communities to be always looking outwards, always subject to the outwards challenge of mission in their practice as well as their aims. Sometimes such prayer groups span churches and act as a means of bringing people together in a positive way. Within the local workings of a mission society I started to challenge the formation of mission support groups based on hierarchical structures as had previously been the case. In its place I suggested the growth of loosely connected 'cell groups' which felt called by God to particular aspects of mission. In other words, the formation of small mission communities that could receive information and help from outside, but which relied more on a common call from God for their existence.

Sometimes support groups arise in places of work and it is not unusual to find local teachers meeting together for prayer and sharing. I have heard of businessmen coming together from within a company or office block to pray and even go through Alpha together. Such groups need to be affirmed as valid mission communities doing a vital work at the cutting edge of mission in this country. Again, ways of linking them with the everyday life of local churches is important. Sometimes mission communities spring into being as a result of the Spirit speaking through world tragedies. In one Midlands church there began a movement of mission to care for Vietnamese refugees that was initiated by the vicar. This became a mission movement within the church with which many identified. But it grew to become a movement alongside the local church with its own full-time staff; now it spans many churches across the country that are linked with many places across the world. Mission communities can grow and change in a way that is both exciting and yet at times unsettling.

Diocesan mission committees do not always get good press in the local church. Yet they can become catalysts for particular mission movements. The mission work in Lichfield diocese was only enabled because of the vision of a mission committee. An established committee can become a mission community if it is freed from the need to try to co-ordinate everything to do with mission and if let loose to be creative in its response to the Spirit. Mission societies were founded as mission communities, but the tendency to become institutionalized and move away from risky mission is always there. Thankfully it is possible to see mission societies as enablers for a plurality of mission movements that span the world. By nature many of these movements will have a rich (and varied!) historical tradition on which to draw. This is an asset in places such as the Sudan where the importance of long-term solidarity with a suffering church is a vital part of mission.

Community, Institution and Mission

I have argued for an emphasis on 'bottom-up' mission as the Spirit prompts the formation of a plurality of mission communities. Such an emphasis does need balancing with an appreciation of the role of church institutions. New communities of the Spirit often see themselves in opposition to the institutional church which they (perhaps correctly) identify as in decline and lacking spiritual energy. The history of the charismatic movement has many examples of the way new communities have broken away from institutions. In turn the institutional church challenges what it sees as an approach to mission that bypasses the church. This may be based on different understandings of 'church' but it is understandable that leaders in the institutional church may feel that their call to mission is being ignored.

It seems obvious that both communities and institutions are required, and I want to suggest some of the more positive interactions that we can aim to foster between them. Timothy Yates has suggested that the voluntary principle represents initiative, flexibility and spontaneity. Hence mission communities can bring new life and a renewed creativity to existing institutional structures. They will challenge the form and necessity of particular structures and ways of working in a way that needs to be listened to by church leaders. This requires an openness by institutions to change and a willingness to listen to those not represented in the power structures of the institution. Mission communities can also bring life to otherwise lifeless, but useful, church structures. Clergy chapters, synods and diocesan committees can be brought to life if connected with mission communities. In the other direction church institutions have a vital role to play in carrying and developing tradition which is needed by mission communities. Such communities need to be ready to acknowledge their limitations and learn from the wider traditions of which they are a part. Institutions also have an important role in fostering partnerships between voluntary communities which can often act like independent entities. For this, communities need to be ready to acknowledge that others have been called by the Spirit to tasks similar to their own. Accountability is something institutions also offer communities and is something needed but not always wanted! Accountability without over-control is a difficult but necessary balance. Within such guidelines a plurality of creative mission movements can develop that are part of the universal church and relate to specific institutions within that church.

5
Conclusion

Charismatic missiology is fuelled by the tradition of Pentecost which emphasizes experiences that bring God and humanity closer together by the Holy Spirit. Such experiences point to God's kingdom, which is holistic in nature, and give birth to mission communities that seek ever more of that kingdom. These communities span the world-wide church and witness to a God who has brought all things together in Christ. There is a theological development in this missiology from the *Spirit* to the *kingdom* to *communities* to the *church*. Underlying the whole of this missiology is the conviction that Christ is Lord over all things. This approach marks a charismatic missiology out from some other approaches to missiology. Underlying this theology is a conviction that any focus on the Holy Spirit cannot but lead us ever outwards in our mission and ever onwards in our thinking. We cannot expect to focus on the Spirit and keep our lives and mission neatly boxed up. The Spirit forever drives us out in mission, beyond the boundaries of our present experience. We need to appreciate more deeply the presence of the kingdom in the present, and yet also let the Spirit lead us on a path towards the future kingdom. There is a forwards movement that is characterized by deepening experiences of the kingdom. Mission is the task of bringing a taste of the future kingdom into the present by the Holy Spirit. It is about the kingdom dynamically experienced now. Mission is about communities of the Spirit grasping a kingdom that is forever moving outwards beyond them. Mission is the natural life of the Christian because it is the natural life of God. May we seek and listen to the Spirit in an ever deeper way in order that our practice and understanding of mission may continue to grow.

6
Bibliography

For detailed academic treatments of Pentecostal-charismatic missiology the following are significant books and articles worth consulting:

Cox, Harvey, *Fire from Heaven: The Rise of Pentecostal Spirituality and the Reshaping of Religion in the 21st Century* (London: Cassell, 1996)

Dempster, Murray W, Bryon D Klaus, and Douglas Petersen, eds, *The Globalization of Pentecostalism: A Religion Made to Travel* (Oxford: Regnum Books, 1999)

Faupel, D William, *The Everlasting Gospel: The Significance of Eschatology in the Development of Pentecostal Thought* (Sheffield: Sheffield Academic Press, 1996)

Hodges, Melvin L, *The Indigenous Church* (Springfield: Gospel Publishing House, 1953, 1976)

Hollenweger, W J, *Pentecostalism: Origins and Developments Worldwide* (Massachusetts: Hendrickson, 1997)

Kärkkäinen, Veli-Matti, '"Truth on Fire": Pentecostal Theology of Mission and the Challenges of a New Millennium' *Asian Journal of Pentecostal Studies* 3: 1 (2000) pp 33–60

Land, Steven J, *Pentecostal Spirituality: A Passion for the Kingdom* JPT Sup, Vol 1 (Sheffield: Sheffield Academic Press, 1993)

McClung Jr, L Grant, 'Missiology' in *Dictionary of Pentecostal and Charismatic Movements*, eds S M Burgess, G B McGee, and P H Alexander (Grand Rapids: Regency reference library, 1988) pp 607–609

McGee, Gary B, 'Pentecostal Missiology: Moving Beyond Triumphalism to Face the Issues' *PNEUMA* 16, No 2 (1994) pp 275–281.

Penney, John Michael, *The Missionary Emphasis of Lukan Pneumatology* JPT Sup, Vol 12 (Sheffield: Sheffield Academic Press, 1997)

Pomerville, Paul A, *The Third Force in Missions* (Massachusetts: Hendrickson, 1985)

For more background to the issues raised in this Grove booklet you might like to refer to the following books and articles:

Allen, Roland, *Missionary Methods: St Paul's or Ours?* (Grand Rapids: Eerdmans, 1912, 1962)

Barrington-Ward, Simon, *Love Will Out* (Basingstoke: Marshall Morgan and Scott, 1988)

Bosch, David, *Transforming Mission: Paradigm Shifts in Theology of Mission* (New York: Orbis, 1991)

Cartledge, Mark J, 'A New *Via Media*: Charismatics and the Church of England in the Twenty-First Century' *ANVIL* 17, No 4 (2000) pp 269–282.

Chan, Simon, *Pentecostal Theology and the Christian Spiritual Tradition.* JPT Sup, Vol 21 (Sheffield: Sheffield Academic Press, 2000)

Dakin, Tim, 'The Accidental Missionary' Paper written at Carlile College, Nairobi, 1998

Fee, Gordon D, *God's Empowering Presence* (Massachusetts: Hendrickson Publishers, 1994)

Lord, Andrew M, 'The Holy Spirit and Contextualization' *Asian Journal of Pentecostal Studies* 4, No 2 (2001) pp 201–213

Lord, Andrew M, 'The Voluntary Principle in Pentecostal Missiology' *Journal of Pentecostal Theology*, No 17 (2000) pp 81–95

Lord, Andrew M, 'Mission Eschatology: A Framework for Mission in the Spirit' *Journal of Pentecostal Theology*, No 11 (1997) pp 111–123

Moltmann, Jürgen, *The Spirit of Life* (London: SCM, 1992)

Sider, Ronald, *Evangelism and Social Action* (London: Hodder and Stoughton, 1993)

Stibbe, Mark, *Revival*, Thinking Clearly Series (Crowborough: Monarch, 1998)

Taylor, John V, *The Go-Between God: The Holy Spirit and the Christian Mission* (London: SCM, 1972)

Walls, Andrew F, *The Missionary Movement in Christian History* (Edinburgh: T&T Clark, 1996)

Warren, Robert, *Being Human, Being Church* (London: Marshall Pickering, 1995)

Wright, N T, *New Heavens, New Earth: The Biblical Picture of Christian Hope* (Grove Biblical booklet B 11)

Yates, Timothy, 'Evangelism Without Hyphens' *ANVIL* 2, No 3 (1985).